CONVERSATIONS

POEMS OF
LIFE AND LOVE

KATHRYN CAROLE ELLISON

Published by Lady Bug Books, an imprint of Brisance Books Group.
Lady Bug Press and the distinctive ladybug logo are registered trademarks of
Lady Bug Books, LLC.

Lady Bug Books
400 112th Avenue N.E.
Suite 230
Bellevue, WA 98004
www.GiftsOfLove.com

For information about custom editions, special sales and permissions, please email
Info@GiftsOfLove.com

Manufactured in the United States of America
ISBN: 978-1-944194-93-2

First Edition: October 2023

A NOTE FROM THE AUTHOR

The poems in this book were written over many years as gifts to my children. I began writing them in the 1970s, when they were reaching the age of reason. As I found myself in the position of becoming a single parent, I wanted to do something special to share with them — something that would become a tradition, a ritual they could count on.

And so the Advent Poems began — one day, decades ago — with a poem 'gifted' to them each day during the Advent period leading up to Christmas, December 1 to December 24. Nearly fifty years later, my kids still look forward each year to the "gifted" poems that continue a family tradition, and that new generations have come to cherish.

It is my sincere hope that you will embrace and enjoy them and share them with those you love.

Children of the Light was among the early poems I wrote, and is included in each of the *Poems of Life and Love* books in The Ellison Collection: (alphabetically) *Awakenings, Beginnings, Celebrations, Choices, Conversations, Gratitude, Happiness, Heartstrings, Horizons, Inspirations, Milestones, Mindfulness, Moments, Possibilities, Reflections, Sanctuary, Sojourns,* and *Tapestry.*

After writing many hundreds of poems, *Children of the Light* is still my favorite. In the process of writing it, the words seemed to spring from my heart, and soul... and flowed so effortlessly that it was written in a single sitting. All I needed to do was capture the words on paper.

"Light," to me represents all that is good and pure and right with the world, and I believed then — as I do today — that those elements live in my children, and in all of us.

We need only to dare.

– KCE

DEDICATION

To My Parents: Herb and Bernice Haas

Mom, you were the poet who went before me.
Thanks for paving the way.
From you I learned to appreciate the power of Poetry.

And Dad (Daddy), you always believed in me,
no matter what direction my life took.
Thank you for your faith in me,
and for your unconditional love.

TABLE OF CONTENTS

LIFE'S JOYS

CONVERSATIONS	3
FREEDOM	5
ON BEING HUMAN	7
THE REAL McCOY	8
KEEPING CHRISTMAS	9
RIGHT OR RIGHTEOUS	10
HUMANITARIANISM	11
THOUGHTS, FEELINGS, ACTIONS	13
VALUE JUDGEMENTS	14
INTERDEPENDENCE	15
TRUE FRIENDS	17
TRAVEL AND ADVENTURE	19
WORSHIP	21

LIFE'S LESSONS

PUTTING FIRST THINGS FIRST	25
TRANSITIONS	26
WORDS... OR NOT	27
IMPERMANENCE	28
POWER	29
RESPECTING DIFFERENCES	31

LIKE WATER FOR LEADERSHIP   33

YOU ARE WHO YOU ARE   35

WAR   36

ACCOUNTABILITY   37

THE TRULY BURNING QUESTION   39

VISION   40

DIPLOMACY   41

REINCARNATION   43

FAITH   45

LIFE'S GIFTS

A MATTER OF PERSPECTIVE   49

IMPERFECT (REAL) FRIENDS   50

EXAMINING PATRIOTISM   51

BEAUTY   53

CHILDREN OF THE LIGHT   55

TRUTH   56

THE SOUL OF A MAN   57

EMPOWERMENT   59

... AND THE CONVERSATION CONTINUES   61

LOVE   63

LIFE'S JOYS

CONVERSATIONS

"The bond of all companionship is conversation," my friends.
"Whether in marriage or friendship," it holds true.
This is wisdom from Mark Twain, who shared his thoughts
With people like me and with people like you.

The art of conversation is the art of hearing,
As well as the art of being heard.
An ideal conversation is an exchange of thoughts,
And not an eloquent exhibition of words.

A real conversation always contains an invitation!
Yes... like an invitation to join in the dance.
You're asking them to reveal themselves to you,
As you reveal yourself to them, with resonance.

Different people can look at the same fact
And interpret it differently, I imagine.
To understand where another is 'coming from?'
Well, that's where conversation begins.

A good conversation can shift the direction of change,
If those on each side are equally heard.
Choose to have a conversation *with* others
Rather than talking *at* them with your words.

FREEDOM

Freedom is not guaranteed to us
Without working for it day after day.
Keeping freedom a fact in our daily lives
Takes responsibility (not meant as a cliche).

As Ronald Reagan so wisely declared,
"Freedom is never more than one generation away
From extinction." That means we didn't inherit
Any genes or blood type that would pave the way.

No, freedom must be fought for, and then protected,
And finally handed on to the next generation...
With the premise that they must carry the burden
Of protecting it for themselves to its next commemoration.

"Education unlocks the door to freedom."
So said George Washington Carver, a learned man.
He understood the degree of responsibility
That comes with freedom. (Do the very best you can.)

Sandra Day O'Connor, the first female Supreme Court Justice,
Stated these words which added to her legacy:
"The freedom to criticize judges and other public officials
Is necessary to a vibrant democracy."

Abe Lincoln weighed in on the subject of freedom:
"America will never be destroyed from [without]."
No, it will come from within, if we allow special interests
To decide what is best, and if we sell ourselves out.

George Washington said, "If the freedom of speech
Is taken away [from our rights],
Then dumb and silent we might be led
Like sheep to the slaughter." (Resist with all your might!)

To be free is not merely to cast off one's chains,
But to live in a way that respects others' independence.
None of us are free until all are out of bondage.
Respond to all dangers with loving intelligence.

ON BEING HUMAN

The old world Romans had a line or two
That in a time of need would see them through.

And when I was a girl of seventeen
I learned a Latin line of which I'm keen.

It goes this way: (It's often said with zest!)
To err is human, "Errare humanum est."

At certain times you'll tend to self-destruct
Because of simple minor misconduct.

Remember your mistakes are transitory,
So learn your lessons and go on to glory.

The second part of this Old Latin line,
Translated, means: "To forgive is divine."

When those around you seem to fail the test,
Forgive them, and do not be distressed.

THE REAL MCCOY

For all there is to do in the world
(And there's a lot, for sure),
We must remember only one thing,
And that's to remain always pure...

Pure in spirit and pure in heart,
No matter how complicated things get.
It's not so much what we do,
But how we do it. And yet,
We sometimes tend to believe that we
Are all the things we do.

We get wrapped up in roles... and then
Our act is limited to
Expectations and images that
Are not the real McCoy.
If we can remember the difference, then
Our hearts will leap for joy.

KEEPING CHRISTMAS

How do we keep Christmas alive in our hearts?
How do we defeat Scrooge each year?
It's so easy at times when we're tired or discouraged
To lose Christmas feelings we hold dear.

We keep Christmas by sinking the shafts of our spirits
Deep beneath the tinsel-y facade,
And renewing within us the season's inner meaning
Of Christ, the son of God.

We rediscover the faith and the simplicity of a child.
We behold everything with new eyes.
We search our hearts and hear angels sing
With music that drifts to the skies.

Keeping Christmas requires us to use some effort,
Requiring discernment and emotion.
By evaluating, rededicating and reaffirming what we know
We will share the love and devotion.

RIGHT OR RIGHTEOUS

(Thank You, Laurens Van Der Post*)

The world can be full of frightening things.
(Like things that go bump in the night).
The unknowns of change can keep one up late
With mind games conjuring images of fright.

And people, too, can be pretty scary
With attitudes of wanting to fight.
Human beings are never more frightening than when
They are positive that they are right.

*Laurens Van Der Post is 20th Century Afrikaner Author, Farmer, War Hero, Political Advisor to British Heads of Government, Close Friend of Prince Charles, Godfather of Prince William, Educator, Journalist, Humanitarian, Philosopher, Explorer, and Conservationist.

HUMANITARIANISM

Who are we, as human beings,
If we ignore the suffering of others, everywhere?
Great minds and great hearts have commented on this,
And have left us with wisdom I wish to share:
If you can't feed a hundred people, feed just one.
It's important that you act, no matter how insignificant.
One act of kindness a day can make a difference.
When you live in an unjust world, you can't remain nonchalant.

Love grows only by sharing it with others
(Sound advice to remember, if you would).
Go into the world and do well, my children,
But also, go into the world and do good!

A person's true wealth is the good he/she does
In the world for others most appreciative.
We make a living by what we get,
But we make a life by what we give.

Humanitarian work is part of your life's goals.
We are faced with inequality, again and again.
The burning questions we should ask ourselves:
"If not us, then who? If not now, then when?"

THOUGHTS, FEELINGS, ACTIONS

If you have a thought and a feeling to match it,
But no action to carry out the impulses there,
You're just spinning your wheels; you're stuck in the mud,
And frustration is present everywhere.

Likewise, you can have a thought and an action,
But without feeling to motivate, it's only a parody.
The action won't last long; you can be sure of that.
Mind sparks the feelings, but feelings move the body.

Then feeling and action, without directed thoughts
Is like a powerboat without a rudder.
It's seen a lot in addictive behavior –
In review it can make you shudder.

In other words, all three must be present –
A corresponding thought and feeling and act –
In order to function in a most positive way;
To build trust and confidence as you interact.

VALUE JUDGMENTS

The more you judge, the less you love.
It's really just as simple as that!
Mother Teresa said, "If you judge people,
You've not time to love them." That's that!

The world you perceive is merely a reflection
Of your own state of mind at that moment.
All it reveals is your own level of consciousness,
And is usually farther from any truth existent.

Voltaire suggested, if one really needs to judge,
To "Judge a man by his questions, not his answers."
We learn more about someone by what he's asking
Than we do from someone who is spouting 'whatevers.'

Remember, whoever sets himself up as a judge
Of TRUTH AND KNOWLEDGE (all in caps)
Will be shipwrecked by the laughter of the gods,
Who will label the judgment as merely "claptrap!"

INTERDEPENDENCE

"Interdependence is a fundamental law of Nature!"
Did you understand the words in the above line?
"Interdependence is a fundamental law of Nature!"
They're the wise words of the Dalai Lama, not mine.

Interdependence means that what affects you directly
Will affect everyone else in an indirect way.
We are all individual parts of a magnificent whole,
Combining our efforts with others' to make headway.

"No man is an island, entire of itself..."
John Donne, a 16th century poet, made this statement.
We belong, all of us, to one human family,
Surrounded by nature and our environment.

The further a person drifts away from Nature,
The less able he is to practice interdependence.
As our independence increases, on the whole,
We do better when others do better; there's evidence.

Interdependence is a decision only independent people can make;
There's no such thing as a self-made man!
We are all made up of thousands of others' inputs –
Kind deeds, or words of encouragement, helps us do what we can.

All people and all things are interdependent.
No nation can solve its problems alone.
We need each other, and the sooner we learn it,
We'll survive the storm together, truth be known.

Resolution of the problem is dialogue, and lots of it,
When people, or countries, or cultures collide.
With honesty and courage, and an ear to listen,
Dialogues occur and differences subside.

We should be evolving with a new world view
That maintains one simple proposition:
That all of nature – humans, animals, earth –
Are interconnected, interdependent, and not in opposition.

TRUE FRIENDS

There are things you know and want to share...
Your ideas about life, large and small.
It's what YOU learn and know to be true
That matters in YOUR life at all.

We each must find our own way, it's true;
We can't ride on someone else's back.
And we can travel in many different styles,
And still stay on our track.

It's nice to know that we have friends
Who are pulling for us all the way...
Who wish us well and who don't require
That we check in with them every day
To report the success or failure of our trek.
They trust that what we're doing
Is absolutely right for us; there's no doubt
That what we've chosen is worth pursuing.

True friends support and don't get caught up in
Every little process we go through.
They know that, like them, we're making our way,
And we'll falter some until we find our path true.

They love us, they accept us, they wish us well,
As we love them, in return.
They share our joys, they bolster our morale;
They love to watch us learn.

And friends like that stay with us through the
Days of our lives; they are tradition.
The others who manipulate and push and prod
Fall by the wayside through natural attrition.

We don't have to dislike the "others" for their ways.
They just don't know a better way.
We can only wish them well, and pray they find
That manipulation doesn't pay.

TRAVEL AND ADVENTURE

"I'm not the same, having seen the moon
Shining on the other side of the [earth]..."
These words from Mary Anne Radmacher
Resonate completely. Travel allows for rebirth,
And a new way to see things, offering new ways to think.
The mind is opened and the soul illumined.
As Steinbeck suggests on the subject of travel:
"Humans don't take trips; trips take humans."

A mind that is stretched by a new experience
Can never go back to its former dimensions.
The life you have led doesn't need to be
The only life you have... a wise contention.

˙Though we travel the world over to find the beautiful
We must carry it with us, or we find it not.˙
Emerson is credited with speaking this wisdom…
It clearly is more than a passing thought.

And finally, Mark Twain weighs in on the subject
Of regretting missed opportunities… (Heaven forbid!):
˙Twenty years from now you'll be more disappointed
By the things you didn't do than by the ones you did.˙

WORSHIP

The art of worship is an inner adventure,
Between you and your God, one on one.
Outer symbols can create mood and environment,
But it's personal when all is said and done.

Worship is meditation and prayer for expressing
The soul's innermost desire.
It's envisioning all that is heroic and good.
It's lifting your spirits higher.

It's cleansing your minds of fear and worry
So love can fill that space
With goodness, kindness, and blessings to bring
Big smiles upon your face.

Worship is counting your blessings... being thankful
For the power to grow and share
The love with others which moves us all forward
To the oneness which is so rare.

LIFE'S LESSONS

PUTTING FIRST THINGS FIRST

Putting first things first sounds familiar and quite simple,
But in actual practice, what does that mean?
Sure, you might have a list of things in mind
To prioritize for your daily routine.

But, take a step back – take the long look at your goal.
Your list may not bring you any closer to your desired end.
Perhaps it's time to rethink about how to proceed
So your goals are reached as you intend.

Do not simply prioritize what is on your schedule
(Your items may prevent your chance to succeed),
But schedule your long-range priorities first
Before you continue to proceed.

With a pared down agenda there's little wasted effort.
You're not wasting your time in a distracting direction.
You always have time for the things you put first.
Believe in yourself, your goals, and your perfection.

TRANSITIONS

You've heard of the proverbial straw, I'm sure,
That put the camel in traction.
Compare it, if you will, to the chain of events
That brought on your own changing action.
Each single event was probably not
The determinate transaction –
Yet transition occurred each step of the way;
Like with the camel, a cumulative reaction.

Transition begins at one place in your life,
And its effects are seen from every angle.
Your positive mindset gives you all you need
So that, from old tapes, you disentangle.
Soon you find yourself reaching farther and farther,
Adopting methods that to you are "newfangled."
The effects of this change reach deep within
And emanate out to every quadrangle.

WORDS... OR NOT

"Words, Words, Words, I'm so sick of Words..."
As in *My Fair Lady*, a Broadway show.
The characters there obsessed on the words,
But didn't always communicate, don't you know?

Words can be confusing, and difficult to use,
Yet they remain the most common way
To communicate with others in daily doings.
Understanding often is in disarray.

More wisdom is present in things–as–they–are
Than in all the words men use each day.
Words are the fog one has to see through.
They can confuse. They can lead one astray.

When people ask for an answer you don't know,
Say nothing. Smile... that is your clue.
And for things you know, you need not explain.
The best and shortest answer is in what you do.

IMPERMANENCE

Everything in life is just for a while.
Our lives are written in disappearing ink.
Life's a continuing dance of birth and death...
A dance of change, of impermanence, I think.

Everything that has a beginning has an ending.
Make peace with that fact, and all will be well.
If you insist on holding on to a 'dying' thing
Your life can become a 'living' hell.

Impermanence is the constant transformation of things.
Without impermanence, there can be no life.
To know this, you've unlocked your door to reality;
And, with your acceptance, you'll avoid unnecessary strife.

The knowledge of impermanence forces us to act,
Knowing each time we do a thing might be the last.
We are no longer content to sleepwalk through life.
Embrace and enjoy it — become an enthusiast!

POWER

In keeping with the feeling of being a part
Of God – your inner spark of the Divine –
Call upon that spark and consider it a force
For you to use as you define.

You've experienced the joy in turning it outward
As your "heart went out" to someone in need;
Or when loving someone – maybe even a pet –
Made you feel as if you were becoming weak-kneed.

The emanation that you feel as your "heart goes out"
Is the power from the all-important God link.
It is the very heart of God moving through you.
It even surpasses your power to think.

Cultivate this power and turn it outward.
Help others with it all you can.
The rewards, unexpected, will amaze and delight.
You end up with more than when you began.

RESPECTING DIFFERENCES

Democracy is not the assumption of leadership
By the few who have won the election;
But is based on the wisdom, the conscience and participation
Of the many who will shape the direction.

It's the give and take in our society that makes
Our nation strong and viable to the rest.
When everyone thinks alike, nobody thinks!
How we work together and communicate is the test.

Divisiveness and making the other person wrong
For having a point of view that differs
From one we hold is not the way to solve
Any problems. It just makes matters worse.

It's not our differences that divide us. Oh, no!
It is our inability to recognize and accept...
That not everyone thinks or believes the same.
Respect for others will win! (What a concept!)

Respect for ourselves guides our morals,
While respect for others guides our manners.
Respecting others' opinions does not necessarily mean
We drop our own, and carry their, banners!

Appreciating the similarities is the first step, I believe,
To communication between opposite opinions;
Then respecting the differences while in discussion...
Giving the relationship the most important attention.

The respect we show to others (or the lack thereof)
Immediately reflects on our own self-respect.
Show respect to people whether they deserve it or not.
It doesn't define their character, but it's yours it does reflect.

Speak your honest convictions and feelings,
And prepare to live with the consequences.
Remember to appreciate your similarities,
And don't forget to respect the differences!

LIKE WATER FOR LEADERSHIP

CONSIDER WATER:
It doesn't ask for papers of breeding
Or demand any qualification.
It simply cleanses and refreshes everything.
Its goal is purification.

It freely and fearlessly goes beneath
The surface in its ebb and flow.
It follows the Natural Law of things –
Sometimes fast, and sometimes slow.

CONSIDER THE LEADER:
He works in any setting without
Complaint as things evolve.
He works with any person or issue
At hand in order to solve.

He acts so all will benefit,
And serves regardless of pay.
Reward for him is reaching the goal
Without undue delay.

His straightforward speech rings fair and true;
You can depend on his not being phony.
He intervenes only to shed new light,
Or now and then to create harmony.

CONSIDER THE COMPARISON:
From watching the movement of water
The leader becomes good at miming,
And knows that action in order to solve
Is dependent upon perfect timing.

Like water, the leader is yielding and gentle
And does not push or shove.
And the group does not resist or resent.
The goals are achieved with love.

YOU ARE WHO YOU ARE

"But, who am I?" you ask yourself,
When you are feeling full of wonder.
The answer comes at different times
To different people who stop to ponder.

The truth is that you are who you are.
There's no getting around this absolute fact.
A better question to ask the universe
Might be, "Where is my purpose, my impact?"

Each of us is uniquely different
From every other human on the earth.
And you must hold to your chance to live
Your own uniqueness. It's yours from birth.

If you are often feeling calm and at peace
And are in touch with your purpose for being,
Then you're living in concert with your true self.
I do not hear you disagreeing.

WAR

The act of war is very wrong.
Overt killing defiles the temple of God.
It shouldn't be done – it goes against
The meaning to your lives, period!

However, when attacked, it is compulsory
To defend that temple. Be brisk.
Never be afraid to strike back when your life
Or your loved ones lives are at risk.

ACCOUNTABILITY

Accountability is the measure of a leader's height.
A leader who is accountable will do things right:
Calling leaders to be responsible before placing blame,
And to realize leading others is not just a game.

Conscience binds and accountability liberates...
Failure to follow through will negatively translate.
Opinion is the lowest form of human knowledge...
Fact-finding and truth-telling will give you an edge.

Unless you're dead, you can keep your promises;
It's easier if you can examine your old prejudices.
Never promise more than you can perform.
Always strive higher – much higher than the norm.

The price of greatness is responsibility,
Which gives your actions a strong sense of credibility.
A leader must be accountable to his nation's laws.
Decisions cannot be made by "drawing straws."

Being reliable is the basis of accountability.
"Walking your talk" illustrates your dependability.
It's always the right time to do things right.
Your actions can be trusted. They are honest and forthright.

Life is better when people keep their word.
When they don't, the meaning of their words becomes blurred.
I strive to be accountable for my thoughts, words and actions.
Being less than honest will spoil all interactions.

The only thing in your way is you,
So check your motives, and push your way through.
You are the reason for your success or failure,
And for most social ills, accountability is the cure.

THE TRULY BURNING QUESTION

It's troubling, you know, to think of one's self
As the center, the be-all, the end,
And then turn around, find another soul there
Who likely could become my friend.

I feel so unique – and I guess I am –
Because there's none other like me anywhere.
But the feelings I feel and the thoughts that I think
Are like those of others – we share!

I must be connected somehow to it ALL
To be able to understand and sense
What others are feeling and experiencing.
The wonder of it is immense.

So let me understand the paradox
(If a paradox is to be understood):
I'm unique as a person, but in the Tree of Life,
I'm just part of the wood.

VISION

There is a path from dreams to success,
And lucky the person who finds it.
With vision and courage, and perseverance –
Plus hard work – you will reap the benefit.

Vision without action is merely a dream;
And action without vision gets you nowhere.
For success, you cannot have just one or the other.
Combine them, for a chance of getting somewhere.

It's said that sight is the function of the eyes,
But vision is the function of the heart.
Your vision will be clear when you've looked deep inside.
Carl Jung implied this wisdom. He was pretty smart!

While we're in the mode of famous words of wisdom,
Helen Keller, herself, shared this assertion:
"The only thing worse than being blind
Is having sight, but [lacking the] vision."

DIPLOMACY

Diplomacy in all of your dealings makes sense.
Why argue to have to establish your position?
As saying the right thing at the right time is treasured,
Avoiding saying the wrong thing always is your mission.

Diplomacy is giving the other person an opportunity
To hand you that thing that you are needing.
It's making a point without making an enemy.
It's making sure the conversation is proceeding.

Diplomacy does not mean you're relinquishing your rights
To an opinion or a stand on any subject.
It means engaging with your counterpart
To address your shared concerns with mutual respect.

Conversation, like machinery, works better when lubricated.
Diplomacy is the magic oil that keeps conversations alive.
To say nothing when listening is half the art of diplomacy.
It's being sensitive to the truth so understanding can thrive.

Be a craftsman in your speech, that you may be strong.
The strength of your tongue is mightier than all fighting.
An ideal diplomat stays true, accurate and calm,
With patience and good temper... Objective? Uniting!

REINCARNATION

The primary goal of living, it is said,
Is to perfect one's soul, before you're dead.
Most times we don't make it before we die,
So our loving God gives us more than one try.
God is all loving, and provides a way
To correct our errors when we stray.
The path to God is varied and hard.
We will stumble and slip and fall backward.
It makes no sense to give it only one try...
To pass or fail... to laugh or cry.
So God brings us back to try it over
To further perfect our soul, and discover
Our paths to reach the levels of perfection.
That, after all, is our main intention.
God does not condemn us to hell
Because we're not "saved." Do not dwell
On stories or threats of wallowing in fire,
Or never being able to escape the mire.

Those stories were born strictly out of fear.
The early Church Fathers feared loss of power.
At an early Council of Nicaea (in agitation)
They burned all references to reincarnation.
In churches we hear about our souls not being saved
Because of some actions where we've misbehaved.
Reaching that level of perfection ordained
By both God and you, it is explained,
Is the true definition of what being saved means.
Remember the agreement – no in-betweens.
Each life brings us close to the perfection we seek.
The errors we correct with special technique.
Eventually no further lives will be needed,
If lessons we learn are particularly heeded.

FAITH

Faith is such an oddball thing to have;
There's little emotion or fact involved at all.
It is beyond description, but for the feelings
Of peace that set the theme for life overall.

When you have faith there is no need to rule
The actions of your fellow humans, or your own.
The need is gone to guide another's life,
And in its place is harmony, before unknown.

LIFE'S GIFTS

A MATTER OF PERSPECTIVE

When someone dies, the common question
Is: "What wealth has he left behind?"
Perhaps it's only curiosity, but
It seems to cross one's mind.

On the other hand, those who greet him –
And that's the angels on high –
Ask, "What good deeds have been sent before him
Before he chanced to die?"

Perhaps the lesson to be learned here is:
Look not at what a man owns;
But look, instead, at what he IS...
Then say a prayer over his bones.

IMPERFECT (REAL) FRIENDS

Peace on earth begins with you,
And the one who bugs you the most.
It's amazing how much you learn each time
You go with him to the post.

If he is always "bugging" you,
Check for "termites" in your own house.
By removing your own annoying quirks
You'll have less cause to grouse.

If you set out to understand another,
As you travel through each doorway;
It's amazing, but true, you'll reap great rewards,
Understanding yourself along the way.

No one is perfect, but should you insist,
You'll experience great resistance.
Take your chance on an imperfect friend;
It's the **only** kind in existence.

EXAMINING PATRIOTISM

"Unhappy the land that is in need of heroes."
    – Bertolt Brecht

Mark Twain said: "Patriotism is supporting your country...
All the time," as he paused in his thought;
Then added: "and your government (only) when
It deserves it!" (A passing shot.)

Teddy Roosevelt said: "Patriotism means to stand by the country..."
Then added a clarification quite sound:
"It does not mean standing by any public official
Unless he or she serves the country." (Words profound!)

The English writer, Julian Barnes, said: "The greatest patriotism
Is to tell your country when it's behaving [badly];"
To make it accountable to all of its people.
Is that happening here at home? No... sadly.

And Edward Abbey, essayist and novelist,
Wrote these words – it's clear what he meant:
"A patriot must always be ready to defend
His country against his government."

Benjamin Franklin uttered this, and somehow it applies
To the present ungainly situation:
"You can give a man an Office," (elected by the people)
"But you cannot give him Discretion."

What we in our country really want
Is an America as good as its commitment.
Our Constitution outlines those promises very clearly.
Are they unfolding in the way they were meant?

Our Constitution is a wonderful gift,
But it has no power on its own.
We, the People, give it meaning. We must participate...
The outcomes are up to us, it has been shown.

BEAUTY

When you think of the word "beauty,"
In your mind's eye, what do you see?
Can it be calculated or measured or even described?
Is it something about which we can agree?

Goethe says, "Beauty is a manifestation
Of secret natural laws,
Which otherwise would have been hidden
From us forever." It gives one pause.

And Khalil Gibran says this about the subject
(He is specific; there is no debating.):
"We live only to discover beauty.
All else is a form of waiting."

Thich Nhat Hanh states: "To be beautiful
Means to be yourself..." no more.
Sophia Loren: "It's how you feel inside,
And reflects in your eyes," therefore.

Trying to pin a definition on beauty
Is like trying to build with sand.
As soon as you think you've found it,
It slips steadily from your hand.

CHILDREN OF THE LIGHT

There are those souls who bring the light,
Who spill it out for all to share.
And with a joy that does excite,
They show the world that they do care.
It is so very bright.

In this sharing, love does pervade
Into their lives and cycles round;
And as this light is outward played
The love is also inward bound.
It is an awesome trade.

You are a soul whose light is shared.
It comes from deep within your heart.
It's best because it is not spared,
Because it's total, not just part.
And I am glad you've dared.

TRUTH

Buddha says, "Three things cannot be hidden:
The sun, the moon and the truth..."
The lesson is strong and should be learned
While you are still in your youth.

Truth is compared to the oil on the water...
The level of the oil doesn't drop,
No matter how much water you add to depress it.
Truth and oil will always float to the top.

Denying the truth does not change the facts.
They are there before you, night and day.
Truth, like the sun, can be shut out for a time,
But it is always there. It won't go away.

Truth exists; only lies are invented.
(I have this on great authority!)
The truth is still the truth, even if no one believes it.
A lie is still a lie, even if supported by a majority.

THE SOUL OF A MAN

"The soul of a man is divided into three parts:
[They are] reason [and] passion and intelligence."*
For all the wisdom the stating of it imparts
Between man and other animals there's a difference.

Intelligence is found in the human animal;
It is found in the jungle and ocean as well.
The dog or the porpoise is not considered abnormal
When it is trained to "speak" or ring a bell.

And other animals are prone to passion,
Or else they surely would become extinct.
Their mating takes place in unique fashion!
(Beyond that it's difficult to be succinct.)

Man has no match in his ability to reason.
In that department he must stand alone.
We think animals function only from season to season,
But man is the only one who must function alone.

* Pythagoras (6th Century BC) a Greek Mathematician and Philosopher

EMPOWERMENT

"Above all, be the heroine (hero) of your life,
Not the victim..." (So says Nora Ephron.)
Rumi says, "You were born with wings...
Why prefer to crawl through life?" Walk On!

There's too much talk about the empowerment of women,
And its importance for improving the world situation.
Its not just women who are lacking empowerment...
Many men, many children, people everywhere face discrimination.

Maya Angelou, in her wisdom, left us with this thought:
(Her words of wisdom make her a gem.)
"You may not control all events that happen to you,
But you can decide not to be reduced by them."

The diarist, Anais Nin, is quoted quite often,
And her comment on empowerment is a guide to overcome:
"And the day came when the risk to remain tight in a bud
Was more painful than the risk it took to blossom."

"Grow through what you go through," shared by Anon Y. Mous
Is another way to describe self-motivated empowerment.
The more you exercise fearlessness, the more natural it becomes.
Do not be run by your fears, but by your accomplishments.

You were put on this earth to achieve your greatest self;
Also to live out your purpose, and do it with courage.
The most courageous act is to think for yourself. Aloud!
Go forth with strength, make it your pilgrimage.

... AND THE CONVERSATION CONTINUES

What is more satisfying than a good conversation
With a person who stimulates your mind, and your heart?
A good conversation can shift your perspective.
People who engage are practicing their art.

Many famous people have commented on the subject;
Anne Morrow Lindbergh enjoyed a good conversation.
She said, "It's as stimulating as drinking black coffee,
And just as hard to sleep after." (Fun association!)

Even with all the modern "Zoom-y" technology
A face-to-face conversation is certainly my preference.
A face-to-face conversation is unfolded slowly.
It teaches patience; moreover, it creates confidence.

Remember that "silence is one of the great arts of conversation."
Cicero related that opinion in his writings.
You listen to their words before you respond.
Give-and-take in conversation is much more inviting.

Ideal conversation is an exchange of thought.
It's not oratory or an exhibition of wit.
You build on another person's words and observations,
And both of you reap the benefit.

True happiness arises from the enjoyment of one's self;
And after that, the company of others that you hold dear.
Friendship and conversation with your select companions
Create in your world a loving atmosphere.

LOVE

Love is force; it is never lost.
It's the perfect emanation of good.
If you put love out into the world
It will be absorbed, as it should,
By someone who needs it at the time,
And who would give it back if they could.

Love always comes back, though you may not see it.
Learn to be open to its call.
Though some may ignore love when it circles,
It leaves an impression, big or small.
Love will always hit its mark
When it's sent in good faith over-all.

You can test it for yourself – Beam a shot of love
To someone with whom you're in contact.
Do they react, does something change?
Sooner or later love will make an impact.
Send love to strangers – a smile or a touch.
It's a wonderful way to interact.

A CLOSING THOUGHT

POETRY

It's the revelation
Of a sensation
That the poet
(Wouldn't you know it)
Believes to be
Felt only interiorly
And personal to
The writer who
... **writes it.**

It's the interpretation
Of a sensation
That was fueled by
A poet's sigh
And believed to be
Shared mutually
And personal to
The lucky one who
... **reads it.**

About the authoR

Kathryn Carole Ellison is a former newspaper columnist
and journalist and, of course, a poet.

She lives near her children and stepchildren and their families in the
Pacific Northwest, and spends winters in the sunshine of Arizona.

You might find her on the golf course, traveling the world, writing poems,
or enjoying the arts in the company of dear friends.

Late bloomeR

Our culture honors youth with all
It's unbridled effervescence.
We older ones sit back and nod
As if in acquiescence.

And when our confidence really gels
In early convalescence...
"We can't be getting old!" we cry,
"We're still struggling with adolescence!"

ACKNOWLEDGMENTS

I have many people to thank...

First of all, my (now) adult children, Jon and Nicole LaFollette, and Jon's wife Eva LaFollette, for inspiring the writing of the poems in the first place... and for encouraging me to continue writing poems, even though their wisdom and understanding, and their compassion, surpasses mine...

And thanks to the rest of my wonderful family that I inherited in 1985 when I married their father, Bill Ellison... Debbie Bacon, Jeff Ellison and Tom Ellison, and their respective spouses, John, Sandy and Sue. They, along with their children and grandchildren, are a major part of my daily living, and I am blessed to have them in my life.

Thank you, good friends, who have received poems of mine in Christmas cards over the years, for complimenting the messages in my poems.

Your encouragement helped to keep me writing and gave me the courage to publish.

I am indebted to Kim Kiyosaki who introduced me to the right person to get the publishing process under way... Mona Gambetta with Brisance Books Group has made the publishing process seem easy. I marvel at her abilities and her good humor, and treasure our friendship.

Thanks to Amy Anderson, Sonya Kopetz, Kerri Kazarba Schneider, and Ingrid Pape-Sheldon, my very first, most creative, public relations team of experts who have helped to carry my poems and my story to the world.

And... finally, thanks to John B. Laughlin, a fellow traveler in life, who encourages me every day in the writing and publishing process.

John, I love having you along for this magical ride.

BOOKS OF LIFE AND LOVE
by Kathryn Carole Ellison